Isaac Asimov's

21st Century

Library of the Universe

The Solar System

Saturn

BY ISAAC ASIMOV

WITH REVISIONS AND UPDATING BY RICHARD HANTULA

Gareth Stevens Publishing
A WORLD ALMANAC EDUCATION GROUP COMPANY

Please visit our web site at: www.garethstevens.com
For a free color catalog describing Gareth Stevens Publishing's list of high-quality
books and multimedia programs, call 1-800-542-2595 (USA) or 1-800-387-3178 (Canada).
Gareth Stevens Publishing's fax: (414) 332-3567.

Library of Congress Cataloging-in-Publication Data

Asimov, Isaac.
    Saturn / by Isaac Asimov; with revisions and updating by Richard Hantula.
        p. cm. — (Isaac Asimov's 21st century library of the universe. The solar system)
    Rev. ed. of: The ringed planet: Saturn. 1995.
    Summary: A description of Saturn, the second largest planet in our solar system, which
includes information on its numerous moons, and spacecraft and probes which study it.
    Includes bibliographical references and index.
    ISBN 0-8368-3241-8 (lib. bdg.)
    1. Saturn (Planet)—Juvenile literature. [1. Saturn (Planet).] I. Hantula, Richard.
II. Asimov, Isaac. Ringed planet: Saturn. III. Title. IV. Isaac Asimov's 21st century library
of the universe. Solar system.
QB671.A83   2002
523.46—dc21   2002021802

This edition first published in 2002 by
Gareth Stevens Publishing
A World Almanac Education Group Company
330 West Olive Street, Suite 100
Milwaukee, WI 53212 USA

Revised and updated edition © 2002 by Gareth Stevens, Inc. Original edition published in 1989 by
Gareth Stevens, Inc. under the title *Saturn: The Ringed Beauty*. Second edition published in 1995
by Gareth Stevens, Inc. under the title *The Ringed Planet: Saturn*. Text © 2002 by Nightfall, Inc.
End matter and revisions © 2002 by Gareth Stevens, Inc.

Series editor: Betsy Rasmussen
Cover design and layout adaptation: Melissa Valuch
Picture research: Kathy Keller
Additional picture research: Diane Laska-Swanke
Artwork commissioning: Kathy Keller and Laurie Shock
Production director: Susan Ashley

The editors at Gareth Stevens Publishing have selected science author Richard Hantula to bring
this classic series of young people's information books up to date. Richard Hantula has written
and edited books and articles on science and technology for more than two decades. He was the
senior U.S. editor for the *Macmillan Encyclopedia of Science*.

In addition to Hantula's contribution to this most recent edition, the editors would like to
acknowledge the participation of two noted science authors, Greg Walz-Chojnacki and
Francis Reddy, as contributors to earlier editions of this work.

Printed in the United States of America

1 2 3 4 5 6 7 8 9 06 05 04 03 02

Contents

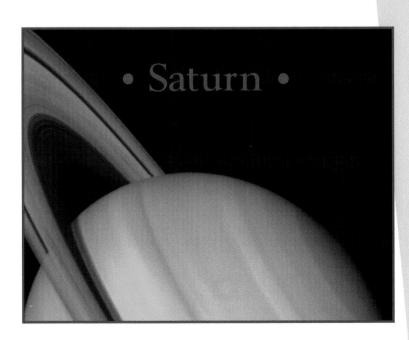

We live in an enormously large place – the Universe. It is only natural that we would want to understand this place, so scientists and engineers have developed instruments and spacecrafts that have told us far more about the Universe than we could possibly imagine.

We have seen planets up close, and spacecrafts have even landed on some. We have learned about quasars and pulsars, supernovas and colliding galaxies, and black holes and dark matter. We have gathered amazing data about how the Universe may have come into being and how it may end. Nothing could be more astonishing.

Within our own Solar System is a world that many people think is the most beautiful object in the sky. It is the giant planet Saturn, with its spectacular rings and numerous moons. Nothing else we can see in the heavens is quite like Saturn. Once you look at it, it is hard to tear your eyes away.

Saturn's Mysterious Handles

In 1610, Italian astronomer Galileo Galilei became the first person to view Saturn through a telescope. Saturn was the farthest known planet at that time. Galileo saw what appeared to be "handles" on each side of the planet. To him it looked as if these handles, which reminded him of ears, disappeared from time to time.

Dutch astronomer Christian Huygens used a better telescope in 1655. Huygens saw that Saturn's handles were actually rings encircling the planet. As Saturn orbited the Sun, Huygens saw the rings at different angles. When he saw the rings from the side, they were so thin that they seemed to disappear. That was why Galileo, whose telescope was not as good, thought the rings sometimes disappeared.

Left: Christian Huygens improved the telescope. He could see that Saturn's "handles" were really rings.

Right and opposite: Galileo did not invent the telescope, but he was the first to use it for astronomy.

The legend of the disappearing ears

The planet Saturn is named after an ancient Roman god. The Greeks called this god Cronus. They believed that he once ruled the Universe. According to the old myths, Cronus was afraid his children would take over his job. So each time a child was born to him, he swallowed the child. His wife was able to save one child, however. When this child grew up, he did indeed take Cronus's place. When Galileo saw Saturn's "ears" disappear, legend has it that he said, "What! Does Saturn still devour his children?"

Inset: Galileo's early sketches of Saturn.

This picture shows how Earth would compare if it could be magically placed between Saturn and Jupiter. You can see why Saturn and Jupiter are known as giant planets.

The Second-Largest Planet

Saturn is the second-largest planet in our Solar System. It is about 75,000 miles (120,000 kilometers) across. This is about 9 1/2 times Earth's diameter. Saturn is about 1/3 as massive as Jupiter and 95 times as massive as Earth. It is located at an average distance of about 886,500,000 miles (1,427,000,000 km) from the Sun. That is 9 1/2 times as far from the Sun as Earth is.

The length of one day on Saturn is under 11 hours. It takes Saturn almost 29 1/2 Earth years to make one orbit around the Sun.

Above: This photograph, returned by a space probe approaching Saturn, shows the planet's bulging middle.

The battle of the bulges!

Although Saturn is much larger than Earth, it turns much more quickly on its axis — once about every 10 1/2 hours. Its middle regions thus bulge outward at the planet's equator. Earth also has a bulge, but it is much smaller.

Earth is only about 13 miles (21.3 km) wider at its equator than at its poles. Saturn is about 7,300 miles (11,800 km) wider at its equator than at its poles, so Saturn actually looks flattened when you look at it through a telescope.

The Only Planet That Floats

If Saturn were hollow, you could pack 763 Earths into it, but Saturn has the mass of only 95 Earths. This means Saturn must be made up of very light materials.

One cubic foot (0.028 cubic meter) of Saturn's material would weigh, on the average, about 43 pounds (19.5 kilograms). This is only about 70 percent as much as a cubic foot of water would weigh. That means Saturn would float on water. If you could imagine putting Saturn on a vast ocean, it would float. As far as scientists know, Saturn is the only world in our Solar System that is lighter than water.

Above: If there were an ocean big enough to put it in, you would see that Saturn could float.

Saturn — a lightweight giant?

The four giant planets are Jupiter, Saturn, Uranus, and Neptune. Jupiter, Uranus, and Neptune all have densities that are about 1.3 to 1.6 times that of water. Only Saturn has a density less than that of water (0.7, or 70 percent, of that of water).

Why is its density only about half that of the other giants? Hydrogen is the lightest of all the elements, and we can say that Saturn contains a higher proportion of it than the other giants do, but that does not answer the basic question of "why."

Unlike Earth, Saturn has
no rocky surface. It has a
deep gaseous atmosphere
and a small core.

Deep Atmosphere

The most common substances in the Universe are the two gases hydrogen and helium. Saturn is made up mostly of these gases. That is why the planet is so light.

When we observe Saturn through a telescope, nothing we see is solid. There is just a thick deep atmosphere.

This atmosphere contains small amounts of certain substances besides hydrogen and helium. These other substances form clouds of many colors. These clouds are the "surface" that is seen when Saturn is viewed through a telescope. Underneath the deep atmosphere, there probably is a small solid core of rock and metal.

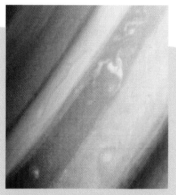

Above: A close-up shows twisted storm clouds and white cloud spots on Saturn.

Above: A 1995 Hubble Space telescope ultraviolet image capturing an aurora on Saturn.

The Hubble Space Telescope tracked an enormous storm near Saturn's equator in 1994.

An artist's conception of Saturn's rings as they arc across a sky thick with clouds. The sunlit rings seem to disappear into Saturn's shadow.

Above: Only a space probe could give us this view of Saturn and its spectacular ring system.

Left: Scientists colored this *Voyager* photo to bring out hard-to-see details in Saturn's many rings.

Ringed Beauty

Saturn is surrounded by rings that circle its equator. The rings are wide but very thin. The brightest parts are about 40,000 miles (65,000 km) wide but less than 650 feet (200 m) thick. This is why the rings seem to disappear when they are observed sideways.

Saturn has two main rings. These are separated by a space that was first noticed by the astronomer Giovanni Cassini. This space is now called the Cassini Division. Outside the Cassini Division is the *A*-ring. On the inner side, closer to Saturn itself, is the *B*-ring. Astronomers have identified several dimmer rings outside and inside these two main rings.

Above: Saturn, its rings, and two of its moons — Tethys and Dione. The gap in the rings is the Cassini Division.

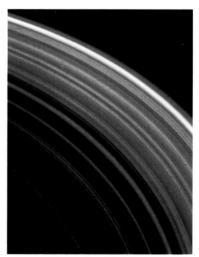

Left: The bright areas in this ring contain more matter than the dark areas.

The planetary ring club — why is Saturn different?

Since 1977, scientists have known that besides Saturn, the planets Jupiter, Uranus, and Neptune also have ring systems. Although Saturn is not the only ringed planet, its rings are the brightest and broadest by far. Why? Scientists cannot say for sure.

A Closer Look

When Saturn's rings are viewed from Earth, they are too far away to show any detail. The *Pioneer 11* probe, which flew by Saturn in 1979, and the two *Voyager* probes, which reached Saturn in 1980 and 1981, allowed a closer look. They revealed Saturn's rings in far more detail than ever before.

The probes showed that what looked like only a few rings are actually tens of thousands of smaller ringlets close together with thin gaps between them. Up close, Saturn's rings look like the grooves of a record album.

Some of the gaps have wavy edges, and one of the ringlets is kinked. Some ringlets separate into two or three parts and appear to be braided.

The rings seem to be made up of pieces of ice and also bits of rock. Some pieces are as small as dust grains and some as large as houses.

Left: Mysterious dark "spokes" skim over Saturn's rings. The spokes may be created by clouds of microscopic particles scattering sunlight.

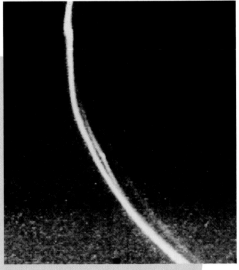

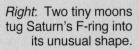

Right: Two tiny moons tug Saturn's F-ring into its unusual shape.

Tens of thousands of ringlets make up Saturn's ring system. This artist's conception of the brightest rings includes the outermost *F*-ring, which has twisted strands.

Scientists think Saturn's magnificent rings consist of dust and small chunks of ice and rock.

Saturn's System of Moons

Saturn has 18 confirmed moons, or natural satellites. In 2000, astronomers reported the discovery of another 12 moons, which will receive official names if they are confirmed. All the moons were discovered with telescopes from Earth or by the *Voyager* probes.

Half of Saturn's 18 confirmed moons are more than 120 miles (200 km) wide. Some of the moons reported discovered in 2000 may be as small as 4 miles (6 km) across.

Saturn's moons are spread over a huge distance. The moon nearest Saturn, Pan, is less than 45,000 miles (70,000 km) above Saturn's cloud tops. The farthest confirmed moon, Phoebe, lies about 8,000,000 miles (13,000,000 km) from the planet, on average. That is about 34 times farther than Earth's Moon is from Earth.

Key to painting (*opposite, bottom*).

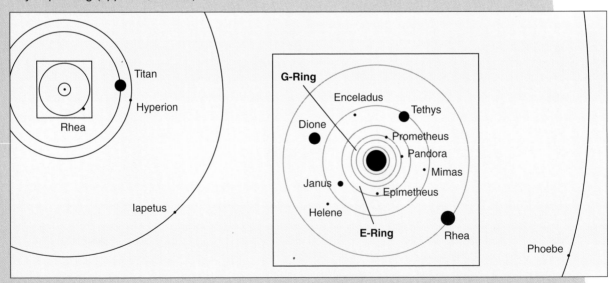

Titan
Hyperion
Rhea

G-Ring
Enceladus
Tethys
Dione
Prometheus
Pandora
Mimas
Janus
Epimetheus
Helene
E-Ring
Rhea

Iapetus

Phoebe

Saturn and its large moons: Dione (*foreground*), Enceladus and Rhea (*top left*), Tethys and Mimas (*bottom right*), and distant Titan (*upper right*).

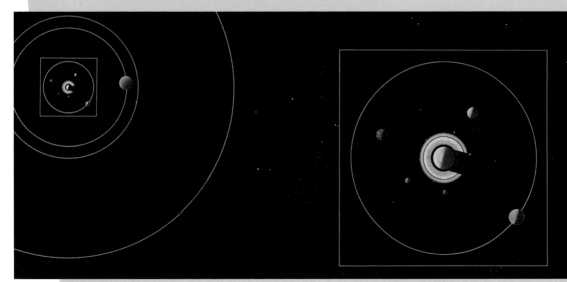

Above: Who's who in the Saturn system? This painting and its key (*opposite page*) show the orbits of Saturn's larger moons.

Above: Something covers up the ice on half of Iapetus, but no one knows what. This painting shows what it might look like where the moon's light and dark sides meet.

Above: This highly detailed picture of Enceladus was taken by *Voyager 2* from 74,000 miles (120,000 km) away.

A Mixture of Moons

Saturn's moons come in many different varieties. Enceladus is about 310 miles (500 km) across, for example. With its gleaming surface, this ball of ice looks as if it were a giant billiard ball.

Iapetus, on the other hand, is about 907 miles (1,460 km) wide. It is the second-farthest of Saturn's confirmed moons. Iapetus might also be a ball of ice, but it is a somewhat dirty one. Iapetus's front side, as it moves around Saturn, is dark, as if covered by dirt. Its rear side, however, is white and shiny. It is a two-toned satellite, but astronomers do not know why this is so.

Left: Iapetus as seen by *Voyager 2*.

Saturn's backward moon

Phoebe, the most distant of Saturn's confirmed moons, is unusual. Most moons in our Solar System always keep the same face toward their planet — this means they turn once around their axis in the time they take to complete one orbit around their planet. Phoebe, however, takes about a year and a half to orbit Saturn, but less than ten hours to spin once around on its own axis. What is more, Phoebe orbits Saturn in the direction opposite to that followed by the planet's other confirmed moons. Why is Phoebe so different? Some astronomers think Phoebe is not an original moon, but a captured comet or asteroid.

Above: Little Mimas has a big crater. Mimas may be small, but it is responsible for the Cassini Division in Saturn's rings. The gravity of Mimas sweeps tiny moonlets out of that region.

Above: This *Voyager 2* image of Tethys clearly shows the big Odysseus impact basin, the biggest crater in the Solar System.

Saturn rises over the rugged terrain of its moon Rhea. The largest craters on Rhea were made long ago when the moon collided with leftover fragments of ice and rock orbiting Saturn.

Cratered Worlds

Many scientists believe that the worlds of our Solar System formed when small pieces of matter smashed together. Today, bodies in the Solar System are still sometimes hit by leftover pieces of matter. If the piece is large, the impact can create a sizable crater.

One of Saturn's moons, Tethys, is about 660 miles (1,060 km) wide and has a crater 250 miles (400 km) across. It may be the biggest crater in the Solar System. Tethys also has a big crack that is dozens of miles wide and stretches about 2/3 of the way around the moon's surface.

Another moon of Saturn, Mimas, is some 240 miles (390 km) across. It has a deep round crater about 1/3 as wide as Mimas itself. Astronomers think the fragment that hit Mimas was almost big enough to shatter the moon into bits. Mimas was lucky to survive!

Left: A crack runs 2/3 of the way around the moon Tethys. Craters large and small pepper the face of this moon of Saturn.

Shepherd and Companion Moons

Several moons are fairly close to Saturn and lie inside or near the rings. Some of them are given the name *shepherds*, because their gravity "herds" the ice grains and boulders that make up the rings, stopping them from drifting too far away and spreading apart. Scientists think the two shepherd moons, Prometheus and Pandora, may be responsible for the unusual shape of the narrow twisted *F*-ring.

At least two tiny moons, each about 15 miles (25 km) in diameter, move in the orbit of Tethys. One, called Telesto, moves ahead of Tethys and the other, called Calypso, stays behind it.

Another moon of Saturn, Dione, has a small companion moon called Helene that moves in Dione's orbit. The moon Janus has almost the same orbit as the moon Epimetheus, and the two moons switch places every four years or so.

Left: Saturn's moon Dione.

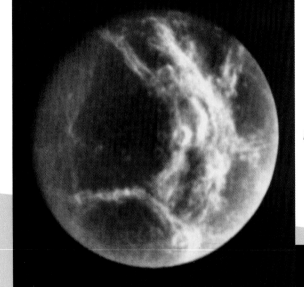

Right: Saturn's moon Dione has a companion called Helene *(pictured)*. Helene travels ahead of Dione in Dione's orbit.

Small moons nicknamed *shepherds* orbit near or within Saturn's rings. Their weak gravity tugs and nudges the particles in the rings, sometimes arranging them into unusual patterns.

Chemicals, such as ethane and acetylene, create smoggy conditions on Titan.

The Giant Titan

By far, the largest of Saturn's moons is Titan. With a diameter of about 3,200 miles (5,150 km), it is bigger than the planets Mercury and Pluto. The only moon in our Solar System bigger than Titan is Jupiter's moon Ganymede.

Titan is the only known moon that has a thick atmosphere.

Its atmosphere is thicker than Earth's, and both are mostly made up of nitrogen. Unlike Earth, whose atmosphere also contains oxygen, Titan's atmosphere contains a fair amount of methane and argon. Sunlight breaks up the methane high above the moon, forming chemicals that create a thick haze – and perhaps even a kind of rain.

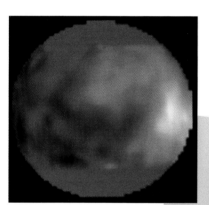

Left: This crude map of Titan's surface was made with the Hubble Space Telescope in infrared light, which is not blocked by the atmosphere.

Above: Titan as seen by *Voyager*, whose cameras could not penetrate the hazy atmosphere.

The Voyage of *Cassini*

Astronomers are curious about Titan's surface. The methane in Titan's atmosphere could, under the action of sunlight, form large molecules of tarlike substances. On Titan's solid surface of rock and ice, there might be rivers, lakes, or even oceans of liquid methane and ethane. In these oceans, there might be islands – or even continents – of tarry sludge.

A spacecraft called *Cassini* was launched in 1997 to explore Saturn and Titan. It is expected to reach Saturn in 2004. Unlike the *Voyager* missions, which just raced past Saturn, *Cassini* will enter orbit around it. That will give scientists more time and opportunity to study Saturn, its complex rings, and its many moons. *Cassini* will also take a very close look at Titan. It has a radar instrument to map Titan's surface, and in 2005, it will drop a probe called *Huygens* into the moon's hazy atmosphere. Stay tuned.

Right: The *Cassini* mission will visit the giant moon Titan during its lengthy study of Saturn.

In 2005, *Cassini* will release the *Huygens* probe. *Huygens* will collect information on Titan's atmosphere as it falls toward the moon's surface.

27

Saturn

The Sun and its Solar System
(*left to right*): Mercury, Venus,
Earth, Mars, Jupiter, Saturn,
Uranus, Neptune, Pluto.

Saturn's larger moons

Confirmed Moons of Saturn

Name	Pan	Atlas	Prometheus	Pandora	Epimetheus	Janus
Diameter*	12 miles (20 km)	19 miles (30 km)	62 miles (100 km)	56 miles (90 km)	75 miles (120 km)	118 miles (190 km)
Distance from Saturn*	83,260 miles (134,000 km)	85,500 miles (137,640 km)	86,600 miles (139,350 km)	88,000 miles (141,700 km)	94,090 miles (151,420 km)	94,120 miles (151,470 km)
Name	Mimas	Enceladus	Tethys	Telesto	Calypso	Dione
Diameter*	240 miles (390 km)	310 miles (500 km)	660 miles (1,060 km)	16 miles (25 km)	16 miles (25 km)	700 miles (1,120 km)
Distance from Saturn*	117,000 miles (188,192 km)	149,230 miles (240,151 km)	184,250 miles (296,513 km)	184,970 miles (297,665 km)	184,970 miles (297,665 km)	234,500 miles (377,400 km)
Name	Helene	Rhea	Titan	Hyperion	Iapetus	Phoebe
Diameter*	19 miles (30 km)	950 miles (1,530 km)	3,200 miles (5,150 km)	160 miles (255 km)	907 miles (1,460 km)	140 miles (220 km)
Distance from Saturn*	234,500 miles (377,400 km)	327,500 miles (527,040 km)	759,200 miles (1,221,850 km)	920,300 miles (1,481,000 km)	2,212,900 miles (3,561,300 km)	8,048,000 miles (12,952,000 km)

* Average width   ** Average distance from Saturn's center

Fact File: Saturn

Saturn is the second-largest plant in our Solar System and the sixth closest to the Sun. A day on Saturn lasts only a little more than $10\,{}^1/_2$ hours. Since Saturn is more than $9\,{}^1/_2$ times farther from the Sun than Earth, it takes Saturn much longer than Earth to orbit the Sun. In fact, a year on Saturn takes almost $29\,{}^1/_2$ of our Earth years.

A close-up of the planet (not shown in the same scale as the moons).

Saturn:
How It Measures Up to Earth

Planet	Diameter*	Rotation Period (length of day)	Period of Orbit around Sun (length of year)	Known Moons	Surface Gravity	Distance from Sun (nearest–farthest)	Least Time It Takes for Light to Travel to Earth
Saturn	74,898 miles (120,536 km)	10 hours, 38 minutes	29.46 years	18+**	0.92***	839–938 million miles (1.35–1.51 billion km)	1.1 hours —
Earth	7,927 miles (12,756 km)	23 hours, 56 minutes	365.256 days (1 year)	1	1.00***	91.3–94.4 million miles (147–152 million km)	— —

* Diameter at the equator.

** Saturn has 18 confirmed moons; a dozen more, reportedly discovered in 2000, still need to be confirmed.

*** Multiply your weight by this number to find out how much you would weigh on this planet; in the case of Saturn, which lacks a surface, the number is for cloud-top level.

More Books about Saturn

DK Space Encyclopedia. Nigel Henbest and Heather Couper (DK Publishing)

A Look at Saturn. Ray Spangenburg and Kit Moser (Franklin Watts)

Saturn. Larry Dane Brimner (Children's Press)

Saturn. Robin Kerrod (Lerner Publications)

Saturn. Elaine Landau (Franklin Watts)

Saturn. Gregory Vogt (Bridgestone Books)

CD-ROMs and DVDs

CD-ROM: *Exploring the Planets.* (Cinegram)

DVD: *The Voyager Odyssey.* (Image Entertainment)

Web Sites

The Internet is a good place to get more information about Saturn. The web sites listed here can help you learn about the most recent discoveries, as well as those made in the past.

Cassini-Huygens Mission. saturn.jpl.nasa.gov/cassini/

Nine Planets. www.nineplanets.org/saturn.html

Pioneer Missions. spaceprojects.arc.nasa.gov/Space_Projects/pioneer/PN10&11.html

Views of the Solar System. www.solarviews.com/eng/saturn.htm

Voyager Project Home Page. vraptor.jpl.nasa.gov/science/saturn.html

Windows to the Universe. www.windows.ucar.edu/tour/link=/saturn/saturn.html

Places to Visit

Here are some museums and centers where you can find a variety of space exhibits.

American Museum of Natural History
Central Park West at 79th Street
New York, NY 10024

Canada Science and Technology Museum
1867 St. Laurent Boulevard
Science Park
100 Queen's Park
Ottawa, Ontario K1G 5A3
Canada

Henry Crown Space Center
Museum of Science and Industry
57th Street and Lake Shore Drive
Chicago, IL 60637

National Air and Space Museum
Smithsonian Institution
7th and Independence Avenue SW
Washington, DC 20560

Odyssium
11211 142nd Street
Edmonton, Alberta T5M 4A1
Canada

Scienceworks Museum
2 Booker Street
Spotswood
Melbourne, Victoria 3015
Australia

Glossary

atmosphere: the gases surrounding a planet, star, or moon. Saturn's atmosphere contains hydrogen, helium, and other gases.

axis: the imaginary straight line around which a planet, star, or moon turns or rotates.

Cassini Division: the space between Saturn's two major rings, the A-ring and the B-ring. It is named for Giovanni Cassini, the Italian scientist who first saw this space.

crater: a hole in a surface caused by a meteor strike or volcanic explosion.

diameter: the length of a straight line through the center of a circle or sphere.

equator: an imaginary line around the middle of a planet that is always an equal distance from the two poles of the planet. The equator divides the planet into two half-spheres, or hemispheres.

Galileo: an Italian scientist who, in 1610, became the first to see Saturn through a telescope.

gravity: the force that causes objects like the Sun and its planets to be attracted to one another.

Hubble Space Telescope: an artificial satellite carrying a telescope and related instruments that has orbited Earth since 1990.

Huygens, Christian: the Dutch astronomer who, in 1655, first identified Saturn's rings.

mass: the quantity, or amount, of matter in an object.

molecules: the smallest particles of a substance.

moon: a small body in space that moves in an orbit around a larger body. A moon is said to be a satellite of the larger body. Saturn has eighteen confirmed moons; the largest is called Titan.

probe: a craft that travels in space, photographing celestial bodies and even landing on some of them.

rings: bands of ice, rock, and dust particles that circle some planets, including Saturn, at their equators.

shepherd satellites: small moons, or moonlets, that orbit within or near Saturn's rings. Their weak gravity helps keep ring matter from drifting out of position.

Solar System: the Sun with the planets and other bodies, such as asteroids, that orbit the Sun.

Voyager: the name of two U.S. space probes that were launched in 1977. Both *Voyager 1* and *Voyager 2* later flew by Jupiter and Saturn. *Voyager 2* also flew by Uranus (in 1986) and Neptune (in 1989).

Index

Born in 1920, Isaac Asimov came to the United States as a young boy from his native Russia. As a young man, he was a student of biochemistry. In time, he became one of the most productive writers the world has ever known. His books cover a spectrum of topics, including science, history, language theory, fantasy, and science fiction. His brilliant imagination gained him the respect and admiration of adults and children alike. Sadly, Isaac Asimov died shortly after the publication of the first edition of *Isaac Asimov's Library of the Universe.*

The publishers wish to thank the following for permission to reproduce copyright material: front cover, 3, 19, 20 (upper right), National Space Science Data Center and the Team Leader, Dr. Bradford A. Smith; 4 (left), AIP Niels Bohr Library; 4 (right), British Museum; 5 (large), The Granger Collection, New York; 5 (inset), Laurie Shock/© Gareth Stevens, Inc. 1988; 6, NASA; 7, Jet Propulsion Laboratory; 8, © Tom Miller 1988; 9, © Calvin J. Hamilton; 10 (upper left), Reta Beebe (New Mexico State University), D. Gilmore, L. Bergeron (STScI), and NASA; 10 (upper right), J. Trauger (JPL) and NASA; 10 (lower), Jet Propulsion Laboratory; 11, © John Foster 1988; 12 (upper), NASA; 12 (lower), Jet Propulsion Laboratory; 13 (both), NASA; 14 (both), Jet Propulsion Laboratory; 15 (upper), © Larry Ortiz 1988; 15 (lower), NASA; 16, Laurie Shock/© Gareth Stevens, Inc. 1988; 17 (upper), NASA; 17 (lower), © George Peirson and Debra Peirson 1988; 18 (upper), © Michael Carroll; 18 (lower), NASA; 20 (upper left), Jet Propulsion Laboratory; 20 (lower), © Joe Tucciarone; 21, NASA; 22 (left), NASA/JPL; 22 (right), NASA; 23, © Julian Baum 1988; 24, © George Peirson 1988; 25 (left), Peter H. Smith of the University of Arizona Lunar and Planetary Laboratory, and NASA; 25 (right), NASA; 26, 27, © Michael Carroll; 28, © Sally Bensusen 1988; 28-29, © Sally Bensusen 1987.